uman

The Essays

First published in Italy
in 2011 by
Skira Editore S.p.A.
Palazzo Casati Stampa
via Torino 61
20123 Milano
Italy
www.skira.net

Printed and bound in Italy.
First edition

ISBN: 978-88-572-0980-7

Distributed in USA, Canada, Central
& South America by Rizzoli International
Publications, Inc., 300 Park Avenue
South, New York, NY 10010, USA.
Distributed elsewhere in the world
by Thames and Hudson Ltd.,
181A High Holborn, London WC1V 7QX,
United Kingdom.

Nick Sullivan

mariner
the call of the sea

SKIRA

One day in 1934, or so the story goes, Hollywood character actor Charles Laughton bowled through the doors of one of the most illustrious addresses in male style. Gieve, then in Bond Street, had been in existence in numerous guises since 1785 (first at 73 The High Street, Portsmouth—the Royal Navy's biggest port) and had built, under its original founder Melchisedek Meredith, a copper-bottomed reputation in the crafting of Royal Navy officers uniforms including the uniform Admiral Nelson wore—and died in—at Trafalgar in 1805. It seemed a pretty good address for the renowned stickler for authenticity to do his nautical costume research. Laughton, you see, was to play Captain William Bligh opposite Clark Gable's Fletcher Christian in *The Mutiny on the Bounty*.

Laughton sailed up to an assistant and asked if the firm would be up to the challenge of creating a uniform correct for the role of Captain Bligh. The salesman disappeared into a back room, emerging after twenty minutes with a dusty ledger listing precisely, in ancient copperplate, the work done by Old Mel, as Meredith had been known in his day, for one William Bligh, RN in 1787, down to the cloth used, the Captain's own measurements and even how much he was charged for his uniform. Laughton, it seems, was satisfied and the rest is Hollywood history.

A garment as suitable for sporting events and day-to-day work, the classic double-breasted coat still owes its existence to the Royal Navy of Bligh's time. It was worn habitually with the fronts buttoned back on themselves, to lie open, revealing white facings.

It was of course navy blue.
The peak lapel remains the only
acceptable lapel for anything double
breasted—simply by nature of the way
such lapels could be buttoned tight
to the neck when properly closed—
to keep out the salt breezes no doubt.
Interestingly the modern Royal Navy
reefer retained buttonholes on both
lapels well into the last century.
At least this much we do know.

Laughton was a fortunate bloodhound.
Just over five years later, in the middle
of September 1940, a direct hit
by an enemy bombing raid reduced the
Bond Street store, a century-and-a-half
of records and almost its entire archive
to smoldering ashes. We might apply
the same pernickety rigor as Laughton
in tracing the double-breasted blazer.
Unfortunately the simple passage
of time has obliterated the history of this

pillar of eternal male style with as much finality as bomb damage. Nearly.

The rest, even the origin of the word "blazer," is much disagreed upon.
But we do know that what we call a blazer should not be called a blazer at all.

Fact 1: the navy double-breasted blazer isn't a blazer at all.
It is a reefer, descended from the reefer jackets worn double breasted and gold buttoned by Royal Navy sailors—initially petty officers—from the middle of the eighteenth century right through to today.
Fact 2: a "blazer" is descended —usually in single-breasted form—from the very bright often luridly striped jackets worn for sports by members of school, university and social organizations from the early

nineteenth century—still seen in all its glory at sports events like Henley Regatta on the Thames and in the uniforms of tonier private schools the world over. The sporting blazer first appeared in England; it gained popularity pretty quickly anywhere a privileged stratum of society had the time and the wherewithal to play games. The term "blazer" was coined in the 1830s for the bright red jackets adopted by the University of Cambridge's Lady Margaret Boat Club. Cut softer and looser than the reefer, it has been harder to assimilate in regular life, by nature of its often eye-popping colors. So for the purposes of debate let us call the double breasted, nautically descended jacket "the reefer," and the single-breasted sports club jacket "the blazer." None of what we do know about the two jackets in question is helped by the growing tendency in modern America and elsewhere, to use the term "blazer" to mean literally anything that resembles a jacket that does not have matching pants. And it's no help whatever to clear discussion to know that the term "reefer" is also used to define the heavier (usually wool melton) double breasted pea-coat that is by all accounts a beefier descendent — for cold weather — of the same original naval jacket. Charles Laughton would turn in his grave. Fortunately there is no room here to dwell on both bloodlines. **So let's keep things strictly nautical.**

The true gold-buttoned, double-breasted reefer occupies a unique place in the sartorial canon. Yet these days it is not a steady one. Too dressy for most men, it is thought too flashy — those shiny brass buttons — for the office.

A suit is far more sensible for work. **The reefer then is neither fish nor fowl, a garment in search of a purpose.**

As a vital piece of Royal Naval uniform, the reefer became the preserve of the gentleman officer, part of his enormous service kit of daily ship-board dress, ceremonial and mess dress that he was expected to purchase bespoke at his own expense. In contrast, the other ranks, or ratings, were decked out from the mid-nineteenth century in a wholly different "square rig" uniform of bell bottom pants (flared legged trousers that were easy to roll up for work on wet decks), jumper and an oversized square-ended blue collar draped over the shoulders.

The moment the reefer escaped its purely naval origins in the late nineteenth century it was easily recognized in civilian life as an exclusively gentlemanly garment; when paired with white flannel pants it was the quintessential rig for waterborne leisure and the summer resort. **At the same time, with the growth of organized sports events, clubs and societies the brightly hued blazer found a market too.**

Gieves & Hawkes might well lay just claim to being the home of the quintessential modern reefer—or at least the British one. For much of the past century and a half Gieve maintained a close symbiotic (and lucrative) relationship with the Admiralty. In 1856 Gieve even dispatched a ship full of tailors, cloth and gold braid as far as the fleet off the Crimea, to guarantee after-sales service to its gentleman customers, even in the teeth of the Russian bear.

The Admiralty, the governing body of the Navy, was at pains from the early nineteenth century to standardize the navy. Until 1857, when universal rules were conceived, officers were left to outfit their crews at their own expense and their own whim, leading to some surprising fashion moments, like the crew of HMS Harlequin, decked out in 1853 by their Captain Wilmott in Harlequin suits. The Admiralty came to rely on Gieve's sartorial expertise to maintain and occasionally update the minutiae governing naval officers uniforms. Gieves, meanwhile, needed the customers and became the officially endorsed destination for the nascent officer. **It was common practice for Gieves to send a letter of congratulations to the parents of any new 14-year-old cadet, so paving the way for a lifetime of bespoke business.**

No "blazers" here: Gieves & Hawkes still politely insists on calling its classic off-the-peg version the "No. 5 reefer, best Barathea." It is not alone: the Royal Thames Yacht Club, Britain's oldest sailing club (est. 1775), in something as essentially twenty-first-century as its website, decrees the dress code for its summer 2010 program of events in one curt, yet loaded, word: "reefers." Military aesthetics are still at the heart of Gieves & Hawkes civilian bespoke and ready-to-wear, "The Gieves chest," the late Robert Gieve said "is a strong chest." **Not lacking in military bearing himself, Gieve was a double-breasted man through and through. His reefers, like his suits, were of course bespoke and all had a trademark robust, fully canvassed torso, suppressed waist and a full skirt, a cut**

14

1 *Costume of the Royal Navy.*
Uniforms of Gunners,
Boatswains and Carpenters,
1830–37

2 *Vincent Van Gogh*
The Mailman Joseph Roulin, *1888*
Oil on canvas, 81.3 × 65.4 cm
Boston, Museum of Fine Arts
Gift of Robert Treat Paine, II
Inv. 35.1982

1

2

3 *When attitude counts: the perfect reefer. Admiral David Beatty (1871–1936), chief commander of the Royal Navy, WWI, 1914–18*

4 *H. R. H. Charles, the Prince of Wales in the 1970s: not quite a nautical setting but definitely an impeccable reefer*

that miraculously enhances the upper body and gives virtual muscle to the shoulders. "I would think every well-dressed man would have at least one," **he told** *The New York Times* **in 1988 as the distinctive double-breasted jacket made one of its periodic resurgences.**

Many of the hallmark garments that are still held as pillars of the gentlemanly wardrobe stem directly from military tailoring and by definition from the officer class. And they are just as much a uniform, designed with subtle details of cut and finish, to set a man apart from—or rather above—other men. The *Preppy Handbook*, which in the early 1980s did much to relaunch the fortunes of the reefer in America, called it the male exoskeleton, placing it firmly in the pantheon of utterly defining Prep garments. Prep's backbone was belonging —having been to the right school, playing squash at the right club, pursuing the right career at the right firm, even driving the right car or walking the right dog. For the American blue-bloods of New England that it affectionately lampooned, the reefer was a badge of belonging, to be worn (off-duty naturally) with loudly patterned or brightly hued trousers called "go to hell pants," a term first coined by writer Tom Wolfe in *Esquire* in 1976.

The early 1980s were certainly a fashionable time to be well bred (or have the money to appear so) on both sides of the Atlantic. *The Official Sloane Ranger Handbook* charted the rise and rise of the Hooray Henry, a tiny strata of upper-class Britain. In Henry's exclusive world, privilege did not necessarily signify money and money certainly did not guarantee privilege. **The double breasted blazer, the *Handbook* said, was a wonderful thing, with conditions... provided you belonged to an obscure cricket club (the Free Foresters), an historic rowing club (Leander), or were a general in the army or over the age of fifty.** Anyone else, it warned, should tread very warily. Even for the *Sloane Ranger* the blazer sailed perilously close to the wind. "A natty blazer with the wrong buttons can slip into caricature," it said with finality.

And it did. When fashion got hold of Preppy and Sloane Rangers, it was the look that defined the decade. The reefer was front and center throughout. Preppy has since become part of the universal middle-class uniform in America, one that is commercial manna while increasingly distant from its blue blood origins.

The exclusive, clubby associations of the classic reefer are at best a double edged sword; it signifies exclusion or belonging, depending of course on your background. What it is not is an egalitarian piece of clothing. But those who spurn the reefer and its associations don't really have a problem per se with the jacket. It's the buttons that cause all the problems.

A college friend was handed down a Savile Row-made wool serge reefer from his grandfather, with a set (complete minus one) of Blackheath Golf Club buttons. He disliked golf, but likes double-breasted jackets—particularly this one, a relic of a beloved relative and which by dint of serendipitous genetics,

fitted him perfectly. Only the single
missing gold button was a catch.
So he returned to the original tailor, still
in business. "Yes," they said. They had
the correct buttons in stock and would
be happy to attach a replacement. All my
friend needed do was to provide proof
of membership of Blackheath Golf Club.
Oh… This was a problem. Blackheath,
the oldest golf club in the world (it claims
foundation in 1608) was then difficult
to get into. In any case he did not have
any intention of taking up golf.
His dilemma was, I've since heard,
resolved a couple of years ago by patient
scanning of eBay. The missing button
was replaced for a tiny sum without need
for passing the stringent requirements
of Savile Row.

Buttons and badges can deceive,
deliberately or intentionally. "Walt" is
slang in the British and American armed

forces (after the fictional fantasist
Walter Mitty) for men who have created
a fictional resume in the military
or (an equal sin) have implied a more
illustrious career than they in fact
enjoyed. Taken to extremes, this can
mean dressing in the insignia
and on occasions the full uniform
of a serving officer or wearing medals
not earned pinned to the chest.
It still goes on today, with a vigorous
upswing since the first and second
Gulf wars. **Not surprisingly, like
the wearing of a regimental tie
to which one is not entitled,
it provokes an extreme reaction
in genuine serving men and
retired soldiers alike.**
While passing oneself off as a serving
officer is considered a cardinal sin
(not to say illegal), no less scorn is
reserved for old soldiers who wear ties
or badges on their jackets on parade days

signifying belonging to units in which they did not serve. There is still more than a whiff of disapproval for simple souls who do no more than wear a fashion blazer with ersatz club badges.

Michael Caine knows his way around a reefer. The lifelong sartorial fan —dressed for the most part by Mayfair's favorite tailor Dougie Hayward— has donned one in numerous roles, not least the comedy *Dirty Rotten Scoundrels* (1988), in which he plays a master con-artist on the Riviera. The tools of his trade are a sharp mind, a regimental tie, flannels and a four-button navy reefer. The veneer of respectability is well rehearsed and it works a treat.
The reefer remains a useful tool lending provenance where perhaps it doesn't naturally belong. Caine's earlier character in *Sleuth* (1972), meanwhile, is Milo Tindle, a working class boy-made-good

and the owner of a string of hairdressing
salons. Yet he looks for all the world
a Gin-and-Tonic-toting member of the
establishment, from the expertly knotted
knit tie to the 6 over 2 reefer (for the
semiotics of buttoning see below).
His nemesis in this dark cat-and-mouse
thriller is Andrew Wyke (Lawrence Olivier),
a genuine country blue-blood with a
withering disdain for the lower classes.
The reefer doesn't fool Wyke for a second.

**Because of its easily donned
mantle of rightness, in the
modern age the reefer is still
fraught with difficulty.
Many love the old-world
associations —the nautical
or clubby vibe of brass buttons
and all—and go straight for
the purest example of sartorial
formality; others find it a stuffy
reminder of being crowbarred**

into theirs at a young age for country- or boat-club parties, of being dressed up and head the other way. For some it's a great way to smarten up jeans and deck shoes, for others it's the height of conformist cheese.

Progress has not helped the reefer. In the democratization of society and the workplace, it has become the short-cut uniform of the petty authority figure, the coach driver or the security officer. It's not for nothing that airline crews still dress like navy officers, albeit in suits made of polyester complete with cuff braid.
It is enough to put one right off.
Of course to those men who truly understand clothes, there is a world of difference between the coach driver and the captain of industry, and nothing that unites their navy reefers.

All jackets are not the same. The difference between men is not marked by what their clothes are called but how well they are made, who made them, and what they are made from.

Progress has also helped it.
Savile Row is not the only authority
on the reefer. Civilian fashion, much
as it adopted the regulated look of the
naval version, has also bent it to suit its
own changing needs. Most noticeable has
been the wholesale increase in comfort
(a fact in all forms of tailored clothing);
technological advances in weaving have
revolutionized fine men's clothes in the
past thirty years and put Italy front and
center in the map of global male style.
It's not just the lightness and softness
of the cloth but also the expertise
of tailors from Naples to Milan who have
given us luxurious ready-to-wear jackets

constructed with no visible means
of support that weigh as little as a shirt
yet drape our imperfect frames with the
requisite degree of patrician chutzpah.

**In Italy and most of Europe,
a blue blazer is suitable office
dress in all but the stuffiest
professions, even with the
Euro-purists' preferred patch
pockets. But like anything else
an Italian man will wear,
it has to be cut like a dream,
soft, yet close to the body,
paired with equally well-cut
charcoal pants—or perhaps
jeans for the true corporate
rebel. In Italy the brass buttons
are usually substituted with
more modest black or navy,
occasionally white. Yet those
sober nautical associations are
still close just below sea level.**

Sticklers for the original nautical heritage
of the reefer—there are many—generally
agree that for nautical correctness
the more buttons there are the better.
In standard tailoring terms,
reefers are described, for example,
as fastening "6 over 3" or "8 over 4;"
the first figure denotes the total number
of buttons in two rows down the front and
the second the number actually
used to fasten the jacket closed on the
wearer's right side. For the Royal Navy
it was always "8 × 4" making for lapels
crossing high on the sternum.
**Was this perhaps the origin
of the term buttoned-up?
Fashion, as interested
in comfort as correctness, has
loosened things up, producing
some interesting anomalies
like the "4 × 1" or (horrors!!)
the "6 × 1," a low slung casual
inflection that makes**

right-thinking purists wince. These gentlemen avert their eyes from such sartorial aberrations and prefer the conservative look yet relative comfort of "6 × 2" or "6 × 3."

Button mathematics aside, anywhere the reefer is worn, one thing is agreed upon. **It can only be in an inky blue black.** Any other color, by definition, means it's a double-breasted blazer and not a reefer. Indigo dyes—though widespread in the Royal Navy well before, were the first to offer a degree of color fastness necessary for the new standardized look set out in the mid-nineteenth century. Such a puritan position in the modern world does not allow for individual expression, or that modern phenomenon that is the fashion designer. But one has to start somewhere, right?

Cloth is key too. Modern, super-light textiles and blends of wool and linen or wool and mohair make gossamer weight reefers a possibility, but can also make for too delicate a look. Worsted serge or barathea is a more traditional choice, but something with a little more texture **—a hopsack or panama weave perhaps, or a piqué— ensures there's no danger of the reefer being mistaken for an orphaned suit jacket.**

There is much gentle disagreement between classic clothiers on the subject of pockets. The naval reefer carries welt or besom pockets with flaps, while the single-breasted version, descended from the blazer normally has three patch pockets. **Nowhere is the patch pocket more rigidly adhered to than in Italy, where one of the marks of a tailor**

**is the perfection with which
he can execute and apply
a patch pocket.**

Style, even such classic style, evolves
a pace at a time, feigning to ignore
fashion but inevitably subject to its
tides. If you're a reefer man you'll find
a thousand variations that work well
enough in a range of situations.
**The perfect modern reefer
is hard to pin down, yet it
resides somewhere between
the deftly crafted suavity of the
Italian and the chesty strictness
of the British version.
For something that is too
dressy for some and too casual
for others, it has been doing a
rather neat balancing act for
nearly two hundred years.**